P9-CSA-353

A GIFT for:

....

FROM:

....

DATE:

....

Looking Up

WHEN LIFE IS LOOKING DOWN

Looking Up

Up

WHEN LIFE IS LOOKING DOWN

Beth Moore

THOMAS NELSON
Since 1798

NASHVILLE   DALLAS   MEXICO CITY   RIO DE JANEIRO   BEIJING

Published in Nashville, Tennessee, by Thomas Nelson, Inc.®
Thomas Nelson, Inc. is a registered trademark.

Published in association with Yates & Yates, LLP, Attorneys and Literary Agents, Orange, CA.

Unless otherwise indicated, Scripture quotations are taken from the *New King James Version.* Copyright © 1979, 1980, 1982, Thomas Nelson, Inc.

Scripture quotations marked ESV are taken from THE ENGLISH STANDARD VERSION. Copyright © 2001 by Crossway Bibles, a division of Good News Publishers.

Scripture quotations marked HCSB are taken from the *Holman Christian Standard Bible,* Copyright © 1999, 2000, 2002, 2003 by Broadman & Holman Bible Publishers. All rights reserved.

Scripture quotations marked NIV are taken from the HOLY BIBLE: NEW INTERNATIONAL VERSION®. Copyright © 1973, 1978, 1984 by International Bible Society. Used by permission of Zondervan Publishing House. All rights reserved.

Scripture quotations marked NLT are taken from the *Holy Bible,* New Living Translation, copyright © 1996. Used by permission of Tyndale House Publishers, Inc., Wheaton, Illinois 60189. All rights reserved.

Scripture quotations marked NASB are taken from the NEW AMERICAN STANDARD BIBLE®, © The Lockman Foundation 1960, 1962, 1963, 1968, 1971, 1972, 1973, 1975, 1977, 1995. Used by permission.

Project Editor: Jessica Inman
Project Manager: Lisa Stilwell
Designed by: DesignWorks Group, Sisters, Oregon

ISBN-10: 1–4041–0514–X
ISBN-13: 978–1–4041–0514–0

Printed and bound in China

www.thomasnelson.com

Table of Contents

Why are you cast down, O my soul?
And why are you disquieted within me?
Hope in God;
For I shall yet praise Him,
The help of my countenance and my God.

PSALM 42:11

Introduction

Life can be excruciating. Crushing, in fact. The sheer magnitude of our worries can press down on our heads and, one inch at a time, we unknowingly descend into a pit of despair. Something so horrible can happen that we conclude we'll never be okay again. We can blow it so badly we think God would just as soon we stayed under that dirt and out of His sight. But if we're willing to let truth speak louder than our feelings and long enough that our feelings finally agree, we can be far more than okay. We can be delivered to a place where the air is crisp, the enemy is whipped, and the view is magnificent.

The Bible teaches that there are no lost causes; no permanent pit-dwellers except those who refuse to leave. Every person can know complete redemption in Jesus Christ, purpose for life, and fullness of joy. No, life won't ever be easy but the trade-off is a spin around Planet Earth that actually means something. I am convinced that when the last chapter of each life story is recorded in the annals of heaven, people would rather have lived out their fullness of days with purpose than without pain.

My life passion is to encourage people to come to know and love Jesus Christ through the study of His Word. My life message within that passion, however, is complete and glorious freedom. The kind only Christ can bring. I do not know why, but it has never been enough for me to be free. I want you to be free too. It is not enough for me to know the thrill of God's presence. I want you to know it too. I want you to know the power of His Word that can defy every addiction, heal any affliction, and plug up every pit. I want you to know a love that is better than life.

I'm writing to tell you that I believe God has scheduled a time and a way for you to get out of your pit. You're going to need to show up for the appointment, though. My prayer is that what follows will serve as an itinerary and guide. If you'll grant me the privilege, I'd like to be your attendant for a while. I've taken this trip before. It's bumpy, but the destination is worth it. Thanks for having me along.

You really can move up and out of that pit.

EVERY PERSON
CAN KNOW COMPLETE
REDEMPTION IN JESUS CHRIST,
PURPOSE FOR LIFE,
AND FULLNESS OF JOY.

I waited patiently for the LORD;
he turned to me and heard my cry.
He lifted me out of the slimy pit,
out of the mud and mire;
he set my feet on a rock
and gave me a firm place to stand.
He put a new song in my mouth,
a hymn of praise to our God.
Many will see and fear
and put their trust in the LORD.

PSALM 40:1–3 NIV

You Know You're in a Pit When...

No matter where we go, a pit can always fit. I'm talking about that shadowy home of the heart, mind, and soul so close and personal that, like mud on a set of tires, we drag it along wherever our physical circumstances move us. On any path we can spin our wheels and throw mud until we dig a ditch right in the middle of an otherwise decent job or relationship. Soon our hearts sink with the dismal realization that we're no better off in our new situation. The scenery around us may have changed, but we're still living in that same old pit.

Let's say that for years you've been living in an old RV so small you can't stretch your legs or stand up straight. Visualize the clutter of too much baggage in too small a space. Imagine the unavoidable odor of the cramped lavatory. Your clothes even start to smell like it. Or is it your hair?

Now, imagine that you've been offered a brand-new home. A real one on a solid foundation with big closets and wide-open spaces. You can hardly wait to move in. Filled with anticipation, you rev up the motor of the old RV and plow it right into the new living room, taking out a wall or two on the way. Ah, finally! A new place to call home! You settle back in your RV seat, take a deep breath, and poise yourself to feel something fresh. Something different.

Then it hits you: that deep breath tasted a lot like that old lavatory. You'd hoped for a change, but your soul sinks with the realization that, though you're somewhere new, everything feels and smells hauntingly familiar.

As disheartening as this realization may be, it could turn out to be the best news you've heard all your life. If it wakes you up to the possibility that every situation you're in feels like a pit because you're taking your pit with you, you've just learned something you really need to know: *you could quit driving around that stinking RV!*

Too often, though, we don't recognize a pit when we're in one. So why would we think we need to get out? One reason some of you nicer folks are in a pit without realizing it is because you mistakenly characterize pits only in terms of sin. In our Christian subculture, we think a pit of sin is the only kind there is. But as we perform a biblical analysis of a pit, we're going to have to think much more broadly than that. We need a way to identify pits and know when we're in them.

So here goes:
You can know you're in a pit when . . .

You Feel Stuck. You'd think enough has already been said about the irony of Christians and substandard living . . . even from my own loud mouth and scrawling pen. I don't know why, but it drives me nuts that people stay in bad places when they don't have to. Jeremiah described his pit as a place of sinking down (38:6). You can take this fact to the spiritual bank: low ground always sinks. There's no living at maintenance level in a pit—that's a big part of what makes a pit a pit.

So they took Jeremiah and cast him
into the dungeon of Malchiah the king's son. . . .
And in the dungeon there was no water, but mire.
So Jeremiah sank in the mire.

JEREMIAH 38:6

You Can't Stand Up. One way you can know you're in a pit is that you feel ineffective and utterly powerless against attack. You can't stand up to assaults, trials, or temptations because your feet are in the mud and mire.

To the ancient Hebrew, a pit was a literal or figurative reference to the grave—to its threat—or to an abyss so deep the dweller within it felt like the living dead. Been there? Me too! You experience what the psalmist experienced and what I certainly experienced: you're in a place "where there is no standing." Drawing from the figurative application, we'll define *pit* this way: a pit is an early grave that Satan digs for you in hopes he can bury you alive. Should you fall into it, make no mistake; he cannot make you stay. Ironically, neither will God make you leave. Like it or not, some things are simply up to us.

I sink in the miry depths,
where there is no foothold.
I have come into the deep waters;
the floods engulf me.

PSALM 69:2 NIV

You've Lost Vision. Unlike that rank old RV, pits have no windows. Scripture paints them as places of darkness. A pit is so poorly lit we can no longer see things that may have once been obvious to us. That's another reason we often stay in the pit. Yes, we can always look up—goodness knows that's the only opening we have—but we're often too focused on our sinking feet to crane our necks to the blinding sky. We can't see out, so we turn our sights inward. After a while, this nearsightedness breeds hopelessness. We feel too buried in our present state to feel passionate about a promised future.

But this is a people plundered and looted,
all of them trapped in pits
or hidden away in prisons.
They have become plunder,
with no one to rescue them. . . .

ISAIAH 42:22 NIV

The good news is, since we are created in the image of God, we are meant to brim over with creativity. Yes, that means *you!* All image-bearers of God were intended to overflow with effervescent life, stirring and spilling with God-given vision. Our imaginations were fashioned like wicks to be ignited by the fire of fresh revelation, dripping with wax that God can imprint with His endless signatures. In the light of God's face shining upon us, we also glimpse reflections of our true selves.

I pray that your hearts will be flooded with light
so that you can understand the
wonderful future he has promised to those he called.
I want you to realize what
a rich and glorious inheritance he has given
to his people.

Ephesians 1:18 nlt

Of All the Ways to
Get into a Pit,
Getting Thrown in—
Not by Some*thing* but By Some*one*—
Can Be the Most Complicated
to Deal With
Emotionally and Spiritually.

When You're Thrown into a Pit

You can get thrown into a pit. That's right, without doing one thing to deserve it and without wallowing your way into it. I'm not talking about a pit of sin here. This one's a pit of innocence—the kind a lot of believers don't realize exists. You can get thrown right into the miry deep before you know what hit you. Or, worse yet, before you know *who* hit you. In fact, those were the very circumstances surrounding the first pit ever mentioned in Scripture. Genesis 37:23–25 records the details:

> When Joseph came to his brothers, they stripped off his robe, the robe of many colors that he had on. Then they took him and threw him into the pit. The pit was empty; there was no water in it.
>
> Then they sat down to eat a meal. . . . (HCSB)

Of all the ways to get into a pit, getting thrown in—not by some*thing* but by some*one*—can be the most complicated to deal with emotionally and spiritually. I'll give you a few reasons why. For starters, when someone throws us in, we've obviously got someone to blame. *It's all that person's fault.* Talk about a scenario with the capacity to eat us alive!

> *For without cause they have hidden their net for me in a pit,*
> *Which they have dug without cause for my life. . . .*
> *My soul shall be joyful in the LORD;*
> *It shall rejoice in His salvation.*

PSALM 35:7, 9

You want to talk complications? Okay, how about times when you've been thrown into the pit by someone else's sin—and that someone happens to be a family member? Or a loved one who was supposed to love you back? Getting over the trauma would have been hard enough had Joseph been thrown into the pit by strangers who picked him randomly. Instead, his own flesh and blood did it—and they did it intentionally. Been there? Me too.

All right, let's twist that rag a little tighter. What about times when a person has been used by the enemy to throw us into a pit, and he or she remains close by, lives on as if nothing has happened (eating, working, playing, going to church, etc.), sees our distress and anguish, but will not hear us? Maybe even despises us for our weakness? Ah, now that's complicated. I know from experience. What's even more tragic is the humiliating lengths we'll go to in order to make someone hear us, and all we end up doing is digging our pits deeper. How often have I made a fool of myself just trying to get someone who hurt me to hear me?

> *Answer me quickly, O LORD;*
> *my spirit fails.*
> *Do not hide your face from me*
> *or I will be like those who go down to the pit.*

PSALM 143:7 NIV

Beloved, I hate to have to bring up this word, but I just don't have a choice. It's the last word any of us want to hear echoing back and forth in a pit we've been thrown into. You already know what this word is, and you're probably sick of hearing it. But we don't want to be like those who hold something against others because they "would not hear," do we? Then we've got to open our ears and hear that difficult word again: *forgive.* It's a tough thing to do, but we've got to forgive, even—no, *especially*—those who don't care to be forgiven.

> *"Now, please, forgive the*
> *trespass of the servants of the God of your father."*
> *And Joseph wept when they spoke to him.*

GENESIS 50:17

I know you've heard all this a thousand times, but this could be the day it sinks in, dear one. This could be the day of your deliverance. You think you can't forgive? I felt the same way. I heard over and over how I'd have to forgive, but in a huff I just folded my arms over my chest and refused to do anything about it. You see, I started out in a pit of innocence, but through the years my bitterness rearranged the furniture until it was nothing more than a well-camouflaged pit of sin. But I thought forgiving my pit-throwers would make what happened all right. But, to be sure, it didn't. Still hasn't. What I didn't understand about forgiveness was that it would make *me* all right. One day I finally began getting the message, and I'm praying right now that this is that day for you.

See to it that no one misses
the grace of God and
that no bitter root grows up to cause
trouble and defile many.

HEBREWS 12:15 NIV

THEN ONE DAY,
at the BOTTOM of MY PIT,
I RAISED MY WEARY HEAD
and DIRTY, TEAR-STREAKED FACE
to the SKY.
AND REDEMPTION
DREW NIGH.

Just Look Up

Think back on Joseph, our first scriptural example of a pit-dweller and one who did not dig his way into it. Somewhere along the way, Joseph decided not only to look up but also to point up. His decision to view God as entirely sovereign and ultimately responsible was not the death of him. It was the life of him. Why? Because he knew God could only be good and do right. The words Joseph spoke over his guilty brothers have been medicine to many sick souls who were willing to swallow them whole: "You intended to harm me, but God intended it for good to accomplish what is now being done, the saving of many lives" (Genesis 50:20 NIV).

Take a good look at that word *intended.* It comes from the same Hebrew word translated "think" in Jeremiah 29:11: "For I know the thoughts that I think toward you, says the LORD, thoughts of peace and not of evil, to give you a future and a hope." God thinks of His children continually. And when God thinks of His children, He only thinks in terms of what can be used toward our good, toward His plan for us, and toward the future. His intentions can only be pure. Right. Full of hope. Promoting peace. Listen carefully. God did not haphazardly or accidentally let Joseph's brothers throw him in the pit. He had already thought it out in advance. Considered it. Weighed it. Checked it against the plumb line of the plan. He had looked at the good it could ultimately accomplish, the lives that could be helped and even saved. Then, and only then, in His sovereign purpose did He permit such harm to come to His beloved child. Had the incident not possessed glorious purpose, God would have disarmed it.

> *And we know that all things work together*
> *for good to those who love God,*
> *to those who are called according to His purpose.*

ROMANS 8:28

Beloved, I don't just know this for a biblical fact; I know it for a personal fact. I live it every single day. Can you think of anything more evil than child abuse? Anything at all? When I was a little girl, God already knew the plans He had for me . . . just as He knew the plans He had for you. In His sovereignty, He allowed a series of wrongs to come to me that had mammoth effects on my life. For many years, I reaped a whirlwind of negative consequences and added insult to injury by piling all manner of sin onto my victimization. Then one day, at the bottom of my pit, I raised my weary head and dirty, tear-streaked face to the sky. And redemption drew nigh. God knew the plans He had for me. Plans to prosper me and not to harm me. Plans to give me a hope and a future. I have lived long enough to see Him accomplish everything His Word says He will. Long enough to see beauty exceed the ashes and divine pleasure exceed the pain.

> *The Spirit of the Lord GOD is upon Me,*
> *Because the LORD has anointed Me*
> *To preach good tidings to the poor;*
> *He has sent Me to heal the brokenhearted . . .*
> *To comfort all who mourn,*
> *To console those who mourn in Zion,*
> *To give them beauty for ashes,*
> *The oil of joy for mourning,*
> *The garment of praise for the spirit of heaviness.*

ISAIAH 61:1–3

Dear one, whether or not I say a word about my past, God uses it every single day without fail in my ministry. In friendship. In motherhood. In marriage.

Oh, beloved, you keep thinking about how things might have been had *that* not happened. But it's your wealth of experience that makes you rich. Spend it on hurting people. They need it so badly. If God can use childhood abuse and family tragedy, He can use anything. You don't have to be in full-time ministry for Him to accomplish the kind of redemption I described above. People in your workplace and your neighborhood are dying for hope. Dying to know there's a future. Dying to know there's a God . . . and that He's *for* them, not against them.

Should you be willing to leave a legacy of faith, some of those lives you help will grace this earth after you're gone. Lives needing the kind of help you can give are surrounding you right now. Each one of them is worth the work.

Now thanks be to God who always leads us
in triumph in Christ, and through us
diffuses the fragrance of His knowledge in every place.

2 CORINTHIANS 2:14

When God
Thinks of His Children,
He Only Thinks in Terms of
What Can Be Used Toward Our Good,
Toward His Plan for Us,
and Toward the Future.

Listen to Me,
you who follow after righteousness,
*You who seek the L*ORD*:*
Look to the rock from which you were hewn,
And to the hole of the pit from
which you were dug. . . .
*For the L*ORD *will comfort Zion, . . .*
Joy and gladness will be found in it,
Thanksgiving and the voice of melody.

ISAIAH 51:1, 3

When You Slip into a Pit

You can slip in. That's the second way you can find yourself in a pit. Unlike the pit we get thrown into, we put ourselves into this one. But here's the catch: we didn't mean to. We just weren't watching where we were going. We got a little distracted, taken in by new sights. The path didn't seem bad; it just seemed new. Exhilarating. We thought we were still okay, but the next thing we knew we were in a hole, our feet ankle deep in mud. The cell phone was dead, and suddenly we didn't have a clue what to do.

Yes, you got into this pit yourself, but it certainly wasn't planned. It wasn't what you wanted. In fact, the possibility of falling into a pit may never have entered your mind. You certainly didn't mean for things to turn out the way they did. You didn't see it coming, but now you're in a hole.

You'd give anything if someone else had thrown you in, because you hate being the one to blame. In fact, at first you tried to think it was somebody else's fault. Anybody else's fault. But then you spent enough time in that pit for the noon sun to peak straight over your head, shedding the first direct light you'd seen from in there. With eyes squinting and a hand cupped on your brow, you looked up to see the marks of two suspiciously familiar heels leaving twin ruts all the way from the mouth of the pit to the bottom where you're now standing. You glance at the back of your shoes and, sure enough, they're caked with mud. That sick feeling in your stomach tells you that—no matter who else was involved—nobody pushed you into this pit. You got yourself into this one. And you're not even sure how.

Of the three ways to get into a pit, I think the one I hate most is getting yourself into it. I hate the fool it makes of you. David hated it too. Empathize with his pain as he looked upon the folly that had brought him to such a low state.

> *My guilt has overwhelmed me*
> *like a burden too heavy to bear.*
> *My wounds fester and are loathsome*
> *because of my sinful folly.*
> *I am bowed down and brought very low . . .*
> *All my longings lie open before you, O Lord;*
> *my sighing is not hidden from you.*
> *My heart pounds, my strength fails me;*
> *even the light has gone from my eyes . . .*
> *Those who seek my life set their traps . . .*
> *I have become like a man who does not hear,*

whose mouth can offer no reply.
I wait for you, O LORD;
you will answer, O Lord my God.
For I said, "Do not let them gloat
or exalt themselves over me when my foot slips."
For I am about to fall,
and my pain is ever with me.

PSALM 38:4–6, 9–10, 12, 14–17 NIV

Traps get set. Feet slip. And I hate how the enemy uses the guilt over how you got into a pit to trap you into never getting out. Hear me clearly: you cannot let him get away with that. Settle in your mind right now that staying in the pit is absolutely unacceptable. Lose it as an option. No matter how responsible and guilty you feel for sliding your way in, God wants you out. If you know Jesus Christ personally, you are not stuck. You do have the power to stand up against the enemy.

It is for freedom that Christ has set us free.
Stand firm, then,
and do not let yourselves be burdened again
by a yoke of slavery.

GALATIANS 5:1 NIV

God still has a vision for you. No matter where you've been, God's full intent is for you to live effectively (see John 15:8) and abundantly (see John 10:10). He loves you dearly, and the fact that you've been foolish doesn't diminish His love one single ounce. Talk to God. Echo the words of the psalmist when he cried:

If I should say, "My foot has slipped,"
Your lovingkindness, O LORD, will hold me up.
When my anxious thoughts multiply within me,
Your consolations delight my soul.

PSALM 94:18–19 NASB

If you don't soak your brain in the truth that you are absolutely secure in the unchanging love of God, you will never feel worthy of getting out of the pit. Satan will keep your feet on slippery ground.

When you want out of your pit, you've got a golden opportunity to see the grace of God as you've never encountered it. Let God's loving-kindness hold you up and ask Him to make His consolations your delight.

For I am convinced that neither death nor life,
neither angels nor demons, neither the present nor the future,
nor any powers, neither height nor depth,
nor anything else in all creation, will be able to separate us
from the love of God that is in Christ Jesus our Lord.

ROMANS 8:38–39 NIV

Using the Hammer of
His Word and the Anvil of
His Unfailing Love,
God Reshaped My Disfigured Desires
Until What I Wanted
More Than Anything on Earth
Was What He Wanted.

When You Jump into a Pit

Y ou can jump in. That's the third and final way you can land in a pit. Before you take the plunge into that pit, you can be well aware that what you're about to do is wrong, probably even foolish. But for whatever reason, the escalating desire to do it exceeds the good sense not to. Unlike the second route into a pit, you didn't just slip in before you knew what was happening. You had time to think, and then you did exactly what you meant to do even if the pit turned out to be deeper and the consequences greater than you hoped.

When all is said and done, you—like me—probably do what you do because you want to. You ordinarily jump into a pit because you like the trip. No, you don't necessarily like the cost but, like all vacations, a great trip can be worth the expense. It looks good. It feels good. Or it tastes good. It just doesn't last nearly long enough, which is why we come back and take the next trip.

Stay with me here, beloved. Surely you know that it takes one to know one. The only reason I'm not still in a pit is because, after many warnings, God mushroomed such devastating consequences of sin and emotional unhealthiness that it nearly killed me—did kill the old me, as a matter of fact. As Job 33:29–30 says:

> *Behold, God works all these things,*
> *Twice, in fact, three times with a man,*
> *To bring back his soul from the Pit,*
> *That he may be enlightened with the light of life.*

God brought me to a place where I was willing to do anything to get out of the pit and everything to stay out. To be out of the mud and mire and have my feet upon a rock became what I wanted more than anything in the world. If you have the same tendency toward pit-jumping, I wish more than anything to talk you into crying out for deliverance before you reach the point I did.

You see, my desires were skewed. In my own pit-jumping (as opposed to pit-slipping), I often ended up doing exactly what I set out

to do . . . what at that moment or in that season I thought I *wanted* to do. Like you, perhaps, I wished I didn't want the things I did. I often hated what I wanted. Still, desire—deformed and destructive—lurched and led. Isaiah 44:20 describes the kind of person I was: "He feeds on ashes, a deluded heart misleads him; / he cannot save himself, or say, / "Is not this thing in my right hand a lie?" (NIV).

I had thought of my heart as only sinful. I didn't realize that deeper still, underneath that film of soil, my heart was sick. One of the most important shifts in my belief system began with the realization that I had a messed up "want to." My desires were tremendously unhealthy. Self-destructive.

*Know then in your heart
that as a man disciplines his son,
so the LORD your God disciplines you.*

DEUTERONOMY 8:5 NIV

Never minimize the power of desire. Though doing what you need to do is the place to start, you'll never make it over the long haul motivated by need alone. The most self-disciplined among us may walk in victory for a few weeks out of the need to do the right thing, but that need will rarely carry us to the finish line. Each of us will ultimately do what we want to do.

Is it any wonder that the first words of Christ recorded in the incomparable gospel of John are "What do you want?" Hear Him echo the same words to you today: "What do you want, child?" What are your secret desires? Place them before Him. Name every single one. No matter how healthy or unhealthy. No matter how respectable. No matter how deformed. I am proof that God can heal the most messed up "want to." In recent years no verse has meant more to me than Psalm 40:8: "I delight to do Your will, O my God; / Your Law is within my heart" (NASB).

Indeed it was for my own peace
That I had great bitterness;
But You have lovingly delivered my soul
from the pit of corruption,
For You have cast all my sins behind Your back.
For Sheol cannot thank You,
Death cannot praise You;
Those who go down to the pit cannot
hope for Your truth.

ISAIAH 38:17–18

I still can hardly fathom that I can say those words and mean them after where I've been. God healed my deformed desires, finally getting through my thick skull that the things He wanted for me were the best things life could offer. Using the hammer of His Word and the anvil of His unfailing love, God reshaped my disfigured desires until what I wanted more than anything on earth was what He wanted. Somewhere along the way, God's law transferred from the stone tablets of my head to the soft tissue of my heart. I bought in—not just spiritually, but emotionally. Jesus finally, completely, won my heart. And if He can deliver me, He can deliver anyone.

> *I will give you a new heart*
> *and put a new spirit within you;*
> *I will take the heart of stone out of your flesh*
> *and give you a heart of flesh.*
> *I will put My Spirit within you and*
> *cause you to walk in My statutes,*
> *and you will keep My judgments*
> *and do them.*

EZEKIEL 36:26–27

FORBIDDEN RELATIONSHIPS

NEVER TURN OUT WELL.

LET ME SAY THAT

ONE MORE TIME: NEVER.

An Automatic Pit

I n my research for this book, I learned that certain kinds of relationships and people become automatic pits for us the moment we intimately engage. For instance, Proverbs 22:14 warns, "The mouth of forbidden women is a deep pit" (ESV). The same is true of forbidden men. A relationship that is so enticing to us precisely because it's forbidden is nothing but a decoratively painted door to a cavernous pit. Scripture could not paint a more vivid picture: their very mouths are deep pits. Place your mouth on one of those and you kiss your solid ground good-bye.

God doesn't just say no because it makes Him feel good about Himself. God feels fine about Himself. If God forbids something, the sooner we believe and confess that it's for our sakes, the better off we'll be. He's actually a yes kind of God (see 2 Corinthians 1:20). You can mark this one down any time and every time: God's no is a quick shove away from a pit.

God cannot be tempted by evil,
nor does He Himself tempt anyone.
But each one is tempted when he is drawn away
by his own desires and enticed.
Then, when desire has conceived, it gives birth to sin;
and sin, when it is full-grown, brings forth death.
Do not be deceived, my beloved brethren.
Every good gift and every perfect gift is from above,
and comes down from the Father of lights,
with whom there is no variation or shadow of turning.

JAMES 1:13–17

Proverbs 23:27 adds that "a prostitute is a deep pit; / an adulteress is a narrow well" (ESV). The King James Version uses a far stronger word than *prostitute*—stronger even than the American Standard Version's *harlot*—and one that suggests that the term isn't limited to someone who is paid to have sex. It refers to anyone who sleeps around and practices immorality as a virtual lifestyle. Needless to say, the verse is equally true in reverse. A man who sleeps around is a deep pit, and an adulterer is a narrow well. Mess with them and, in a manner of speaking, you'll hurl yourself into the bowels of the earth with such meteoric force that only God can pull you out. I don't care how flattering someone's attention may be. If he or she is immoral or married to somebody else, an intimate relationship of any kind with that person will automatically—not probably or eventually—hurl you into a pit. ETA? Instantaneously.

> *Whoever digs a pit will fall into it,*
> *And he who rolls a stone*
> *will have it roll back on him.*

PROVERBS 26:27

Based on everything the Word of God says and everything I've experienced, heard, or observed, I promise you that forbidden

47

relationships never turn out well. Let me say that one more time: never. The pit is deep and dark. And before you know it, you'll find that you are in it all alone.

I've also lived long enough and listened hard enough to become convinced that we are almost always right, no matter how we don't want to be, when we get a nagging feeling somewhere down inside that a person to whom we're growing increasingly attached has a serious dark side. That's the Holy Spirit warning us. Learn to associate darkness with a pit. I say all of this to you out of deep love and concern. Repent and run.

My son, if sinners entice you,
Do not consent. . . .
Do not walk in the way with them,
Keep your foot from their path;
For their feet run to evil,
And they make haste to shed blood.

PROVERBS 1:10, 15–16

A Relationship
That Is So Enticing
to Us Precisely Because
It's Forbidden Is Nothing
But a Decoratively Painted Door
to a Cavernous Pit.

The LORD is my rock and
my fortress and my deliverer;
My God, my strength,
in whom I will trust;
My shield and
the horn of my salvation,
my stronghold.

PSALM 18:2

You Can Get Out

Regardless of whether you were thrown in, you slipped in, or you jumped in, you can get out. And I do mean *you*. I'm not talking about the person who seems to deal with her pit better than you do. We don't need to deal with our pits. We need to get out of our pits. You can do it. Even if you have a history of failed attempts. Even if you don't think you deserve it. Even if you've never lived anywhere else.

But here's the catch: you can't get yourself out. Try as you may, you will never successfully pull yourself out of a pit. Not the kind the Word of God is talking about. Remember the number one characteristic of a pit? Mud and mire. The quicksand kind that gulps your feet whole. You're stuck. As much as you'd like to, as self-sufficient as you'd like to be, as smug as it would make you, you can't do this one alone. Somebody else has to come to your rescue. But there you have options. You can opt for human help or you can opt for God.

To actually see our deliverer could be a decisive advantage. To have an audible conversation would be great. To know that someone really was listening would help. To see the look on a face or hear the tone in a voice—now, to us, that would be real help.

But help alone is not what we're talking about. God meant for people to offer one another a helping hand. The trouble comes when we insist upon someone who is as human as we are becoming our deliverer. Another person—rare though he may be—can pull us out of a pit, but—for the life of him—he can't set us free.

People can help us but they can't heal us. People can lift us but they can't carry us. On occasion people can pull us out of a pit, but they cannot keep us out. Nor can they set our feet upon a rock. When we come out of a pit, if our idea of stability is standing on another human's shoulders, that person's clay feet will inevitably crumble and we'll take a tumble. The job's too big for anyone.

The everlasting God, the LORD,
The Creator of the ends of the earth,
Neither faints nor is weary.
His understanding is unsearchable.
He gives power to the weak,
And to those who have no might
He increases strength.

ISAIAH 40:28–29

Since pit-dwelling is primarily a state of mind, effective deliverance also takes the ability to read people's minds, because what we say often doesn't match where we are. Only God can hang with us through the length and depth of our need. And the length and depth of our baloney. Maybe I'm just talking about myself, but whether or not I realized it, I usually found a way to frame my pit to make me look like a victim. Not only is God omniscient, but His Word is "sharper than any double-edged sword" (Hebrews 4:12) cutting our baloney so thin He can see straight through it. He knows when we're kidding others. He knows when we're kidding ourselves. Knowing all we are, all we feel, and all we hide, God overflows with love and willingness to deliver us. Even after Israel sought the help of the Egyptians, inviting the chastisement of God, Isaiah 30 testified, "Yet the LORD longs to be gracious to you; / he rises to show you compassion" (v. 18 NIV).

"Longs to be gracious." I like the ring of that. We're also repeatedly told that God's love endures forever, which means the Lord is gracious for *long*. That's what former pit-dwellers like me must have. We need a Deliverer who is in for the long haul. Philippians 1:6 tells us that God, who began a good work, is faithful to complete it. Frankly, work doesn't get harder than pit-dweller pulling. Man, who may begin a good work, wears out too fast to finish it. And rightly he should. It's not his job. True deliverance takes some time, some titanic effort, and more patience than the best of people possess. You and I need a strong arm and a long arm.

Therefore, say to the Israelites:
"I am the Lord, and I will bring you
out from under the yoke of the Egyptians.
I will free you from being slaves to them,
and I will redeem you with
an outstretched arm and with
mighty acts of judgment."

Exodus 6:6 niv

You Can Get Out. And I Do Mean *You.*

But Here's the Catch:

You Can't Get Yourself Out.

We Need
a Deliverer Who Is in for
the Long Haul.
Philippians 1:6 Tells Us That God,
Who Began a Good Work,
Is Faithful to Complete It.

When I Begin to Cry Out,
Confess, and Consent
by Speaking God's Word Out Loud,
I Soon Feel the Power
of His Spirit Start to Fill Me Up
from the Tip of My Toes to
the Top of My Head.

The Three Steps Out of Your Pit

Y ou can opt for God. The beautiful thing about opting for God is that you are opting for everything He brings. Because He is infinite, you will never reach the end of all He offers of Himself. Nothing on earth is like fully engaging with God. *Nothing.* God's love is better than life. No one compares.

If you're willing to engage God as your deliverer from the pit, the full-throttle relationship you develop with Him will be the most glorious thing that has ever happened to you. Far more glorious than the deliverance itself. If you're willing. Here comes the challenge. Here's the deal: God wants everything you've got. Every egg in one basket. All your weight on one limb. This very moment He has His fingers gripped on your chin, saying, "Right here, Child. Look right here. I am your Deliverer. There is none like Me."

God will be your complete Deliverer—or nothing at all. That's the one rule of divine rescue.

My soul, wait silently for God alone,
For my expectation is from Him,
He only is my rock and my salvation;
He is my defense;
I shall not be moved.
In God is my salvation and my glory;
The rock of my strength,
And my refuge, is in God.

PSALM 62:5–7

With that one unwavering rule established, let's get busy. To get where we want to go, we need a comprehendible, biblical how-to. I believe the Bible proposes three steps for getting out of the pit, and each involves your mouth:

- Cry out
- Confess
- Consent

It all begins with a cry. And the kind the psalmist was talking about erupts from the deepest part of a person's soul as if his or her life depends on it. This kind of cry can come either from the desperate "I *need* God and God alone" or the deliberate "I *want* God and God alone." Remember, we don't always have to wait until we're desperate. We can wise up enough to know how desperate we'll be if we don't cry out immediately. Either approach, regardless of how it sounds to human ears, rises to the throne of God with the volume of a foghorn in a shower stall. *Cry out.* Open your mouth, say, "God, help me!" and mean it.

> *But from there you will seek the LORD your God,*
> *and you will find Him*
> *if you seek Him with all your heart*
> *and with all your soul.*

DEUTERONOMY 4:29

After you cry out, *confess.* Think sin, but then think wider. Though it's absolutely vital, confessing sin is not the only way we practice confession. In its widest sense, confession is our means of baring our heart and soul before God. Confession is a way we agree with what God says about Himself and about us. Confession takes place every time you tell God how much you need Him. So tell Him what's on your mind. What kind of mess you're in. Who's in it with you. What's holding you back. Who's broken your heart. Even if your first impulse is to think it's Him. As long as you can feel it, spill it. Psalm 145:18 says, "The LORD is near to all who call on him, / to all who call on him in truth" (NIV).

Confession, by the way, is incomplete until we actively accept God's certain forgiveness. Take a fresh look at 1 John 1:9: "If we confess our sins, He is faithful and just to forgive us our sins and to cleanse us from all unrighteousness." And 1 John 3:21–22: "Dear friends, if our hearts do not condemn us, we have confidence before God and receive from him anything we ask, because we obey his commands and do what pleases him" (NIV).

"If our hearts do not condemn us." Our self-condemning hearts can't block our forgiveness, but they can keep us from feeling forgiven. The result will be a twisted resignation to our own capacity to sin rather than any confidence in God's capacity to restore us.

The third step is *consent.* I love this one. Consent is the most beautiful part of the process of getting out of a pit. There is no ambiguity about this step: God wants you out of that pit. He wants you in victory. So all you have to do is *consent* to what He already wants for you.

Beloved, God's will is for you to get out

of that pit. If you will consent to the process and wait upon God as He begins shifting, shoving, and rearranging things for your release, you can go ahead and start getting excited, because it *will* happen. Just as God promises in His Word. If you're ready to start actively consenting, I'm ready to tell you the most effective way to do it.

When I first introduced the three steps to you—cry out, confess, and consent—I told you that each of them involves your mouth. So we're going to learn to speak out. And I don't mean mumbling under your breath. I want you to learn to cry out, confess, and consent using God's Word—and to do so, when at all possible, *out loud.* Volume is not the point. All you need is to have your own ears hear it. Why? I feel so strongly about this concept that I'm almost standing up at the keyboard to write it. Listen, beloved, "faith comes from hearing, and hearing by the word of Christ" (Romans 10:17 NASB). Your faith will be built by hearing your own voice speak the words of Christ.

I can feel totally hopeless in a situation, but when I begin to cry out, confess, and consent by speaking God's Word out loud, I soon feel the power of His Spirit start to fill me up from the tip of my toes to the top of my head. *Faith comes from hearing, and hearing by the word of Christ.* My faith returns, and holy passion burns.

If you'll allow me, I'd like to give you a jump start so that you can get on with the process. At the back of the book, you'll find scriptures I've rewritten into prayers for you. You'll see that these Scripture Prayers don't have to be used word for word. What's vital is that we echo the principles of Scripture so our confidence can grow in a situation because of the certainty that we're praying God's will.

I'm so proud of you for getting this far into this book. I want so badly for you to be victorious, and I know you can be. God's Word tells me you can. I also know that this system works. You have the power of the entire Godhead behind you. You have the Father's will, the Son's Word, and the Holy Spirit's way. What more could you need?

And, anyway, what do you have to lose except a pit? So start making some noise. I bet, when all is said and done, you end up having a mouth as big as mine.

Praise the LORD, O my soul;
all my inmost being, praise his holy name.
Praise the LORD, O my soul,
and forget not all his benefits—
who forgives all your sins
and heals all your diseases,
who redeems your life from the pit
and crowns you with love and compassion,
who satisfies your desires with good things
so that your youth is renewed like the eagle's.

PSALM 103:1–5 NIV

GOD DOES NOT MAKE
HIS HOME IN A PIT.
BOUND TO HIS HOLY ROBE,
NEITHER WILL YOU.

Waiting on God for Deliverance

God can deliver the most hardened criminal or the most hopeless addict in one second flat. With His eyes closed and His hands tied behind His back, if He has a mind to. I know people who made themselves at home in a pit a hundred feet deep and a thousand days long and, seemingly without warning, experienced the instantaneous deliverance of God. One moment they were in the throes of habitual sin—and the next moment they were free as birds.

Maybe God had marked His calendar for a little instantaneous deliverance. I never doubt He can do that. I'm utterly elated when He does. Those are the kinds of testimonies that launch our faith to the moon and bring our congregations to their feet, cheering madly. I love it. I love to hear it. I love to see it.

But I have not experienced it one time. Let me say that again. Not one time. Not even an instantaneous deliverance from something comparatively shallow like a mini-pit of some kind I dug with a soupspoon instead of a shovel. I won't even be heel deep, and still I'll rarely walk away without a fight.

We proclaim him, admonishing
and teaching everyone with all wisdom,
so that we may present everyone
perfect in Christ. To this end I labor,
struggling with all his energy,
which so powerfully works in me.

COLOSSIANS 1:28–29 NIV

I'm telling you, God and I work hard together. Maybe you consume a fair amount of divine energy yourself and, if so, perhaps we could sift some mutual encouragement out of the aggravation of never doing anything easily. I've come to the elementary conclusion that, to God, *together* is the whole point of any process.

Before man was created, God just said something and it happened. "Let there be light" and all. He could still do that. Sometimes He still does. But you might notice that a lot of that instantaneous action ceased after man came along—and obviously on God-purpose. Suddenly God wasn't so sudden. Time became the vehicle for this wonderful thing called history. You could neither rush it nor slow it. All you could do was ride it. And what a ride it was for all those who preceded us.

And what a ride it is for us now. God etches history not on lands and nations but on human lives. Not on superhumans. Not even on particularly impressive humans. God seems to summon the most faithless of all to faith. He is drawn to weakness, perhaps the ultimate proof that opposites really do attract. History unfolds through the encounters and experiences of men and women God calls to know Him. Calls to trust Him, often under nearly impossible circumstances. People prone to wander, prone to bruising, prone to doubting, prone to losing.

For it is the God who commanded light
to shine out of darkness,
who has shone in our hearts to give
the light of the knowledge of the glory of God
in the face of Jesus Christ.
But we have this treasure in earthen vessels,
that the excellence of the power
may be of God and not of us.

2 CORINTHIANS 4:6–7

Think about it. God could have accomplished in an instant many of the things that He decided instead to hammer out over the tedium of years. Sarai could have felt Isaac kick lustily within her before the dust of Ur was off of Abram's sandals. God takes His own sweet time because sweet time is God's to take. Still, if man weren't around, I personally think He'd go back into the instant-action mode. Why wait if there's no one to wait with you? God created time for man. In fact, the words *in the beginning* mark the tick of the first clock. The Trinity has no such bounds in the eternal state. A wait is time oriented and, therefore, primarily man oriented. Perhaps among a host of other reasons, I think God often ordains a wait because He purely enjoys the togetherness of it.

And you must never fear that God is not at work while you wait. He's doing what no one else can. Get a load of Isaiah 64:4:

> *Since the beginning of the world*
> *Men have not heard nor perceived by the ear,*
> *Nor has the eye seen any God besides You,*
> *Who acts for the one who waits for Him.*

If your eyes could only see how God is moving all those chess pieces around the board for maximum impact, it would blow your mind. He's up to something big that doesn't only affect you. He's also after those around you. Furthermore, He's not just interested in impacting the present. He is the One "who is and who was and who is to come, the Almighty" (Revelation 1:8). Within every "is," God is mindful of what "was" and what "is to come," and He intends to show Himself mighty in all of the above.

One thing is certain: you can't accuse God of being shortsighted.

While you wait for God to work and to manifest your sure deliverance, wrap yourself around Him as tightly as you possibly can. Ask Him to make you more God-aware than you have ever been in your life. Bind yourself to Him with everything you've got so that you will ultimately—inevitably— go anywhere He does. Hang on for dear life and never let go. No matter how long it takes, He'll never run out of breath or stop to soak His aching feet. Pin yourself so close to Him that you can almost hear Him whisper. His words will live in you and you will live in Him. God does not make His home in a pit. Bound to His holy robe, neither will you.

> *But those who wait on the LORD*
> *Shall renew their strength;*
> *They shall mount up with wings like eagles,*
> *They shall run and not be weary,*
> *They shall walk and not faint.*
>
> ISAIAH 40:31

WITHOUT HESITATION
GOD OFFERS YOU
a FIRM PLACE to STAND,
but YOUR FEET ARE
NOT FIRMLY SET in PLACE
UNTIL YOU'VE MADE
UP YOUR OWN MIND THAT'S
WHERE YOU WANT to BE.

Make Up Your Mind

So how do you know when the wait is over and you're finally out of that pit? Psalm 40:2 describes one way:

He lifted me out of the slimy pit,
out of the mud and mire;
he set my feet on a rock
and gave me a firm place to stand. (NIV)

One way you know you're out is when you realize after all the slip-sliding and skydiving you've done, your feet are finally planted on a rock, and you've got a firm place to stand. It means you've found a steady place where you can stand all the way up and rest your whole weight on your feet without fear of eventually discovering you're knee-deep in new quicksand. Even if the mountains fall into the sea, you're secure. Even if the seas overtake the shores, you're not going anywhere. Winds may blow and waters rise, but you will not lose ground. Praise His steadfast name, God is not a divine rug someone can pull out from under your feet.

God can hold your weight—the full emotional, spiritual, mental, and physical poundage of you—sixty seconds a minute, sixty minutes an hour, twenty-four hours a day, seven days a week, 365 days a year for the rest of your life.

I want to emphasize that phrase *the rest of your life*. God is not just a firm place to stand. He's a firm place to stay. This book is not about getting out of the pit for a while. It's about getting out of the pit for good. And if that's what we want, we've got to do something absolutely crucial: we've got to make up our minds. The ground beneath our feet will be only as firm as our resolve. As long as we're wishy-washy, what's under us will be wishy-washy too. God *gives* us a firm place to stand, but we have to decide we want to take it. John 3:16 tells us that "God so loved the world that he gave his only Son" (ESV), but He doesn't force anyone to take Him either. God is ever the Giver (James 1:17) but, by His sovereign design, each individual gets to exercise the prerogative as to whether or not to be a taker.

I consider everything a loss
compared to the surpassing greatness of
knowing Christ Jesus my Lord,
for whose sake I have lost all things.
I consider them rubbish, that I may gain
Christ and be found in him,
not having a righteousness of my own
that comes from the law,
but that which is found through
faith in Christ. . . .

PHILIPPIANS 3:8–9 NIV

We take the firm place God gives when we make up our minds and plant both our feet. That's exactly what the Hebrew word translated "firm" in Psalm 40:2 (NIV) means. In another psalm it is used to characterize man's response to God. Psalm 78 speaks of a generation who:

would put their trust in God
and would not forget his deeds
but would keep his commands.
They would not be like their forefathers—

a stubborn and rebellious generation,
whose hearts were not loyal to God,
whose spirits were not faithful to him.
(vv. 7–8 NIV)

You see that word *loyal*? It comes from the very same Hebrew word as *firm*. God's complaint with the Israelites in Psalm 78 was their inability to make up their minds about Him. Were they with Him or not? Like us, they wanted God when they were in trouble, but as soon as the pressure let up, they wanted to chart their own course and be their own boss. The momentary revelry of their rebellion turned into terrible bouts of captivity and consequences. They experienced what we do: the slide into the pit is the only thrill. From that point on, a pit's just dirt.

For if we died with Him,
We shall also live with Him.
If we endure,
We shall also reign with Him.
If we deny Him,
He also will deny us.
If we are faithless,
He remains faithful;
He cannot deny Himself.

2 TIMOTHY 2:11–13

At its very core, loyalty means a made-up mind. That's how God is about you. He's *firm.* He made up His mind about you before the foundation of the world. Regardless of who has betrayed you and what promises they didn't keep, God is firm in His commitment to you. Circumstances don't cause Him to rethink His position. Even if you, like me, have made multiple trips to the pit, His affection for you is unwavering. He's all yours if you want Him. The Rock is yours for the standing. Without any hesitation God offers you a firm place to stand, but your feet are not firmly set in place until you've made up your own mind that's where you want to be. He will not force you to stand. And He most assuredly will not force you to stay.

I'll tell you why I'm hammering the point. Until you finally make up your mind that you're cleaving to God and you'll be calling upon His power from now until Hades freezes over, your feet are set upon a banana peel. You may stand while the wind is calm, but when the storm hits and the floodwaters rise, the undertow will leave you gulping for air.

Through the LORD's mercies
we are not consumed,
Because His compassions fail not.
They are new every morning;
Great is Your faithfulness.

LAMENTATIONS 3:22–23

Life on Planet Earth consists of one crisis after another. Beloved, this I promise you. Circumstances will offer unceasing invitations back to the pit. If your victory depends on the right circumstances, you may as well wave the white flag and surrender to defeat. Just go ahead and take that snort. Gulp that fourth gin and tonic. Binge and purge that pizza, a side of garlic bread, and half gallon of mint chocolate chip. Sleep with that jerk again. Eat, drink, and be miserable.

Or you could make up your mind that you're in with God, standing upon that rock, for the rest of your days. The apostle Paul called it being found in Christ (see Philippians 3:9). No matter how long it's been since you've seen me, He is where you can find me. Whether my health flourishes or fails, that's where I'll be. Richer or poorer, I've made up my mind. In the light of day or dark of night, find me in Christ. Spouse or not. Kids or not. Job or not. I've made up my mind.

When you've made that decision and given your heart, mind, and soul in all their fissured parts; and when you've given your past, present, and future "to Him who is able to keep you from stumbling" (Jude 24); and when you know you're absolutely in, come what may . . . congratulations, sweet thing. You're out of the pit and your feet are on a rock.

Having a firm place to stand doesn't mean life isn't hard and temptations don't come. It doesn't mean you get everything right.

It doesn't mean you don't sin, although you won't be able to wallow in it like you used to. It just means you've determined your position no matter what comes your way. You may sway back and forth. You may curl up in a ball or buck like a bronco. But you've decided where you're putting your feet. And once you're there, it's a mighty firm place to stand.

All Your works shall praise You, O LORD. . . .
Your kingdom is an everlasting kingdom,
And Your dominion endures throughout all generations.
The LORD upholds all who fall,
And raises up all who are bowed down.

PSALM 145:10, 13–14

WINDS MAY BLOW
AND WATERS RISE, BUT YOU
WILL NOT LOSE GROUND.
PRAISE HIS STEADFAST NAME.
GOD IS NOT A DIVINE RUG
SOMEONE CAN PULL OUT FROM
UNDER YOUR FEET.

There's Nothing Quite
Like Trying to
Stay Out of the Pit
while Others Close to You
Are Still in It.

Be Brave

Here's the pitiful truth, as well as I know how to tell it: there's nothing quite like trying to stay out of the pit while others close to you are still in it. I don't think I have to tell you that a whole family can take up residency in a deluxe-sized pit with personalized compartments. So can a whole set of friends. Yep, right there on 105 South Pit Drive. Looks like a house. Acts like a pit. Make no mistake. A pit is an excellent place for a pileup.

If you're the first one who escapes a family pileup, you'd think your fellow pit-dwellers would be happy that at least you got out. You'd think your deliverance would give them hopes of their own, but for some reason that's often not the way it works. Usually when you get out of the pit, somebody in the family feels betrayed that you felt a change was necessary. They think it means you're saying something is wrong with the rest of them. Sometimes when a person decides to have a mind made up toward God and feet firmly set upon a rock, loyalty to Him is misinterpreted as disloyalty to family.

Though my father and mother forsake me,
the LORD will receive me.
For the LORD loves the just
and will not forsake his faithful ones.

PSALM 27:10, 37:28 NIV

Actually, nothing has the potential for greater positive impact in a close-knit group of people than when one decides to break tradition and pursue another level of wholeness. I am convinced that health can be even more contagious than infirmity. Until the breakthrough comes, however, and the Jesus-virus catches, you better glue your feet to the God-rock. The pressure to resume your old rank can be titanic.

Cooperating with God through painful relationship transitions may be the hardest work of all in our deliverance from the pit. Persevere with Him and trust Him—not just with your life, but also with their lives. Despite what they say, you weren't doing them any favors by staying in the pit with them. Keep your feet upon that Rock no matter how plaintively beloved voices call from the pit and beg you to come quickly. Just as you waited upon God for your own deliverance, wait upon Him for theirs. Pray hard for them. Love them lavishly, but do so as a Rock-dweller, not a fellow pit-dweller.

As you accomplish such an impressive feat, don't let the enemy tempt you into developing a prideful spirit because you're out and they're still in. Pride is the fastest track back. Through Christ alone "we have access by faith into this grace in which we stand" (Romans 5:2). Your commitment from this new position to those still in the pit has never been more vital.

Therefore we were buried with Him
through baptism into death,
that just as Christ was raised from the dead
by the glory of the Father,
even so we also should walk in newness of life.

ROMANS 6:4

Then again, not everybody is family; not every tie of the heartstring is God's will; and not every relationship needs to change. Some of them need to end. Just flat end. I don't know a nice way to say this. Some relationships won't survive your deliverance from the pit. And most of them don't need to.

You discover that the pit was all you had in common and that, under different circumstances, you wouldn't even have been drawn together. We can hope that this person is not your spouse. If it is, however, start seeking God for a miracle just as Keith and I did. But if it's not a relationship God blesses and not one His Word binds you to, it needs candid examination.

Ask yourself something I've had to ask myself in my pursuit of freedom: Which of your relationships are fueled by genuine affection and which are fueled by addiction? Or at what point did one transition from the former to the latter? I don't know about you, but I've done exactly what the apostle Paul accused the Galatians of doing. I've started

relationships in the Spirit that somewhere along the way veered into the flesh (see Galatians 3:3). Regardless of how we began, we can become as emotionally addicted to a relationship as to a substance.

Beware of anyone who tries to become indispensable to you. Who becomes the one to whom you repeatedly say, "You're the only person on earth I can possibly trust." If that's really true, then you're not getting out enough. In fact, I'd be willing to bet that he or she is the biggest reason you're not getting out. Boldly identify any "pusher" in your life, anyone who keeps feeding the unhealthy part of you because it feeds the unhealthy part of her. Or of him. Question an inability to be alone. Is it possible that God can't even get to you because of that person? As we near the end of this journey together, I beg you to let no one "love" you to death.

Be strong and of good courage,
do not fear nor be afraid of them;
for the LORD your God,
He is the One who goes with you.
He will not leave you
nor forsake you.

DEUTERONOMY 31:6

Be brave, beloved. Be brave! Do the hard thing. Let that person go if that's what God is telling you. Keith once said to me that saying good-bye is a necessary life skill. Exercise it with a confidence only God can give you and don't beat around the bush when you do. Has He not commanded you? "Be strong and of good courage; do not be afraid, nor be dismayed, for the LORD your God is with you wherever you go" (Joshua 1:9). Say good-bye to that pit once and for all. Living up in the fresh air and sunshine where your feet are firm upon the Rock and your head is above your enemy's is not for the fainthearted.

It's for those who make up their minds.

Watch your life and doctrine closely.
Persevere in them,
because if you do,
you will save both yourself
and your hearers.

1 TIMOTHY 4:16 NIV

Be Brave!

Do the Hard Thing.

Let That Person Go If

That's What

God Is Telling You.

It Doesn't Matter
Whether You Have a
Beautiful Voice or Make
Mostly Noise,
You Were Born for Song.
Your Heart Beats to
the Rhythm of a
God-Song.

Singing a New Song

You will have a new song in your mouth, a hymn of praise to your God. That's the second way you'll know you've waved good-bye to the pit. Right after the psalmist tells us that God sets us on the rock and gives us a firm place to stand, he tells us God gives us a new song: "He put a new song in my mouth, / a hymn of praise to our God" (Psalm 40:3 NIV).

Every one of us was born for song. It doesn't matter whether you have a beautiful voice or make mostly noise, you were born for song. And not just any kind of song. Your heart beats to the rhythm of a God-song, and your vocal chords were fashioned to give it volume.

And they sang a new song, saying:
"You are worthy to take the scroll,
And to open its seals;
For You were slain,
And have redeemed us to God by Your blood."

REVELATION 5:9

Beloved, a song of praise freely sung and spontaneously offered is one of the most blatant trademarks of joy in tribulation. You have not let that situation get to you entirely and bury you in a pit until you've lost your God-song. Likewise, you know you're out of that pit when not only have your old songs returned but something fresh has happened. God has put a new song in your mouth. A brand-new hymn of praise to your God.

I remember vividly every detail in my ascent from the worst pit of my life. Still in acute emotional pain from the situation I'd been in, I was driving home from church by myself on a winter night ablaze with brilliant stars. Singing at the top of my lungs with the praise music blaring from my car speakers, I slid back my sunroof and screamed over and over, "I am free!" I was a long way from being out of pain but, make no mistake, I was out of that pit, and I knew—I absolutely *knew*—I was not going back.

Oh, sing to the LORD a new song!
For He has done marvelous things;
His right hand and His holy arm have
gained Him the victory. . . .
Shout joyfully to the LORD, all the earth;
Break forth in song, rejoice, and sing praises.

PSALM 98:1, 4

Having a new song in our mouths doesn't necessarily mean we've learned three verses to a brand-new hymn replete with a chorus we've never heard before. It could happen that way. You could come out of a season of difficulty where a new contemporary Christian song or a praise-and-worship chorus becomes the expression of a fresh wave of love and awareness of Christ. Sometimes during worship at my church, when the band begins a song that holds significance to me, I want to glance up toward heaven and say to Jesus, "They're playing our song."

When that happens, it's a wonderful moment, but it's not what the psalmist means. He means that a whole new level of praise erupts from a delivered soul. It's as if a lid pops off of an undiscovered canyon somewhere deep inside, and a dam of living water breaks, rinses, and fills it. A testimony of God's goodness springs from the well to the lips.

Music comes alive and suddenly puts words to what you feel. You have a song on your heart that can't help but find its way—in various words and melodies—to your mouth.

As He was now drawing near
the descent of the Mount of Olives,
the whole multitude of the
disciples began to rejoice and
praise God with a loud voice for
all the mighty works they had seen . . .
And some of the Pharisees called
to Him from the crowd,
"Teacher, rebuke Your disciples."
But He answered and said to them,
"I tell you that if these should keep silent,
the stones would immediately cry out."

LUKE 19:37, 39–40

Music is as eternal as the Holy Trinity, ever attempting to fill God's boundless space with infinite echoes of majesty. The Father, Son, and Holy Spirit were surely the originators and trio emeritus of three-part harmony. According to Holy Writ, they apparently considered that something as marvelous and miraculous as the creation of Planet Earth needed accompaniment. Since each member of the Trinity would be busy doing the actual work, they shared the gift of song with others who would in turn play the divine score on perfect cue.

The songs of heaven are unceasingly sung—and never more vividly than when a person like you or like me is being delivered. Please sit up a little, shake the numbness from your head, and pay some extra mind as you read something else that the psalmist testified to his God:

> *You are my hiding place;*
> *you will protect me from trouble*
> *and surround me with songs of deliverance.*

PSALM 32:7 NIV

If that's true—and God Himself says it is—some of those very songs are playing right now. In fact, according to that Scripture, this whole book and every other one like it must be set to music we can't hear. Can you possibly think that God would deliver you in your real-

93

life drama—a drama that engages both heaven and earth—without powerful accompaniment? Without poundings of percussion in the fury? Without weeping violins in the melancholy? Without trumpets of God in the victory? Without instruments you've never seen and sounds you've never heard? Not on your life. The originator of surround sound, God chases you down with melody and hems you in with harmony until your raptured soul finds liberty and your aching feet find stability. Christ, the King, the Creator of the Universe, seeks and surrounds *you* with songs of deliverance.

Can you let that truth sink into your swollen soul? Can you allow yourself to feel that loved? That sought? That significant?

If you've been in a pit, God wants nothing more for you than deliverance, and He has surrounded you with accompaniment on your journey out. Take it seriously. No, take it joyfully. Gloriously!

Speak to one another with psalms,
hymns and spiritual songs.
Sing and make music in your heart
to the Lord, always giving
thanks to God the Father for everything,
in the name of our Lord Jesus Christ.

EPHESIANS 5:19–20 NIV

You Know You're
Out of That Pit When
God Has Put a New Song
in Your Mouth.

God Wants Nothing More for
You Than Deliverance,
and He Has Surrounded You with
Accompaniment on Your
Journey Out.

EARTH AS WE KNOW IT
WILL COME TO AN END,
AND GOD
WILL USHER INTO
EXISTENCE A NEW HEAVEN AND
NEW EARTH WITH
PROPERTIES BEYOND
OUR WILDEST IMAGINATION.

Our Pit-Less Future

Life leaves us in the dark about so many things. When we're little, we think we know what we want to be when we grow up, but when we're grown, many of us no longer have a clue. We walk down an aisle and promise "till death do us part," but God only knows who will part first. Our babies take their first steps across the floor just to get to us, but we have no idea where life will really take them—or if they'll still like us when they get there. We're diagnosed with chronic diseases and coldly told the survival rates, but we have no clue where our number will fall in those statistics. We watch the news and squirm with the fresh realization that a sound mind isn't necessarily a requirement for becoming a world leader. We wonder how in heaven's name some maniac hasn't lost his mind and blown up the planet yet. We blow our hair dry and wonder if we're contributing to global warming. If we live long enough and stay plugged in enough, we end up asking the same question our grandparents and parents asked: *What's this world coming to?* And we shake our heads as if no one has any idea.

God left a lot of questions unanswered—primarily, I imagine, because "without faith it is impossible to please Him" (Hebrews 11:6).

I think He also happens to like surprises. However, what this world is coming to is not unanswered. According to Revelation 21, earth as we know it will come to an end, and God will usher into existence a new heaven and new earth with properties beyond our wildest imagination.

But as it is written:
"Eye has not seen, nor ear heard,
Nor have entered into the heart of man
The things which God has
prepared for those who love Him."

1 Corinthians 2:9

Most folks agree that heaven is a better option than hell—but, comparatively speaking, only a handful of Christians really look forward to their future there. Face it. We're scared to death that it's going to be like our church services, but instead of getting out at noon, it will last an eternity. For the life of us, we can't picture how anything holy can possibly be lively. Let alone fun.

A few years ago I was studying Revelation 7 for a series I was teaching, and God brought back to my mind a familiar Old Testament passage using the same metaphor found in the passage I had just read. A wonderful contrast jumped off the page at me and sent my imagination whirling. See it for yourself. The first passage refers to life on earth. The second refers to life in heaven.

Psalm 23:1–3 says:

The LORD is my shepherd;
I shall not want.
He makes me to lie down in green pastures;
He leads me beside the still waters.
He restores my soul.

Revelation 7:17 says, "For the Lamb at the center of the throne will be their shepherd; he will lead them to springs of living water" (NIV).

Get a load of that: still waters on earth, but springs of living water in heaven. Compared to the white-water existence we'll have in heaven, here we're like toads perched on a lily pad in a stagnant pond. Despite our expectations, heaven is where all the action is. Our present existence, replete with every sunrise, sunset, season change, mountain range, forest glen, and foaming sea, is a mere shadow of an unthinkable reality.

Christ lives in you.
This gives you assurance
of sharing his glory.

COLOSSIANS 1:27 NLT

But in the days when
the seventh angel is about to
sound his trumpet,
the mystery of God
will be accomplished,
just as he announced to his
servants the prophets.

REVELATION 10:7 NIV

I dearly love a great ending to a story, and you need to know that we will get one. The Author of our faith knows how to finish it. As we wrap up this book on getting out of the pit, I want you to know what happens to the devil when all is said and done. It's such poetic justice. Revelation 20:1–3 describes it:

> Then I saw an angel coming down from heaven,
> having the key to the bottomless pit and a great chain
> in his hand. He laid hold of the dragon, that serpent
> of old, who is the Devil and Satan, and bound him for
> a thousand years; and he cast him into the bottomless
> pit, and shut him up, and set a seal on him.

There you have it. Before the Lord does away with Satan once and for all, He's going to give him a taste of the pit. It's the perfect plan, really. And sublimely scriptural. After all, Psalm 7:15–16 promised long ago that:

> *He who digs a hole and scoops it out*
> *falls into the pit he has made.*
> *The trouble he causes recoils on himself;*
> *his violence comes down on his own head.* (NIV)

In God's economy, those who dig a pit for others will invariably fall into it themselves (see Psalm 57:6). God writes perfect endings. He can't help it. He's a wordsmith if you'll ever meet one. Every beginning will have a fitting ending. After all the dirt the prowling lion has gathered in his paws digging pits for us, he will eventually find himself caged in a pit. Maybe the reason his pit is so deep is because God is scooping it out until it reaches the total depth of all the ones the devil dug for us. By the time Satan looks at life from a bottomless pit, our feet will forever be firmly set upon a rock. The air will be clear. The view, crystal. The fellowship, sweet. And the sufferings of this present time won't even be worthy of comparing to the glory revealed to us (see Romans 8:18). We'll ride raftless in rivers of living water and then bask in the Son.

Until then, life on this battered earth will not be easy, but we never have to make another bed in the bottom of a pit.

You will guide me with Your counsel,
And afterward receive me to glory.
Whom have I in heaven but You?
And there is none upon earth that I desire besides You.

PSALM 73:24–25

COMPARED TO THE
WHITE-WATER EXISTENCE WE'LL HAVE
IN HEAVEN, HERE WE'RE LIKE
TOADS PERCHED ON A LILY PAD
IN A STAGNANT POND.

GOD WRITES PERFECT ENDINGS.
HE CAN'T HELP IT.

"Heal the brokenhearted,
To proclaim liberty to the captives,
And the opening of the prison to those who are bound...
To comfort all who mourn,
To console those who mourn in Zion,
To give them beauty for ashes,
The oil of joy for mourning,
The garment of praise for the spirit of heaviness;
That they may be called trees of righteousness,
The planting of the LORD, that He may be glorified."

ISAIAH 61:1–3

Scripture Prayer

CRY OUT

I call to You, Lord, who are worthy of praise, and I am saved from my enemies. The waves of death swirl about me; the torrents of destruction overwhelm me. The cords of the grave coil around me; the snares of death confront me. In my distress I call to You, Lord; I call out to my God. From Your temple You hear my voice; my cry comes to Your ears (2 Samuel 22:4–7). O, my Strength, come quickly to help me (Psalm 22:19). Reach down from on high and take hold of me; draw me out of deep waters. Rescue me from my powerful enemy and from foes who are too strong for me (Psalm 18:16–17). Bring me out into a spacious place; rescue me, Lord, because You delight in me (Psalm 18:19).

CONFESS

S earch me, O God, and know my heart; test me and know my anxious thoughts. See if there is any offensive way in me, and lead me in the way everlasting" (Psalm 139:23–24 NIV). [When applicable . . .] Father, I want to acknowledge my sin to You. I don't want to cover it up. I will confess my transgressions to You, Lord, and You will forgive the guilt of my sin (Psalm 32:5). I confess that You are my Rock, my Fortress, and my Deliverer; You are my Rock, in whom I take refuge, my Shield and the Horn of my Salvation. You are my Stronghold, my Refuge, and my Savior—save me from anything that seeks to destroy me (2 Samuel 22:2–3).

Add any of your own words . . .

CONSENT

You are my lamp, O LORD; You turn my darkness into light. With Your help I can advance against a troop; with You I can scale a wall. As for You, my Father, Your way is perfect; Your Word is flawless. You are a shield for all who take refuge in You. For who is God besides You? And who is the Rock except You? (2 Samuel 22:29–32). If You are for me, who can be against me? You did not spare Your own Son but gave Him up for me. How will You not also, along with Him, graciously give me all things? (Romans 8:31–32). You know the plans You have for me, O God. Plans to prosper me and not to harm me. Plans to give me a hope and a future (Jeremiah 29:11). Thank You, God, for Your willingness to lead me to triumph (2 Corinthians 2:14).

Add any of your own words . . .

Psalm 40

I waited patiently for the LORD;
And He inclined to me,
And heard my cry.
He also brought me up out of a horrible pit,
Out of the miry clay,
And set my feet upon a rock,
And established my steps.
He has put a new song in my mouth—
Praise to our God;
Many will see it and fear,
And will trust in the LORD.

Blessed is that man who makes the LORD his trust,
And does not respect the proud, nor such as turn aside to lies.
Many, O LORD my God, are Your wonderful works
Which You have done;
And Your thoughts toward us
Cannot be recounted to You in order;
If I would declare and speak of them,
They are more than can be numbered.

Sacrifice and offering You did not desire;
My ears You have opened.
Burnt offering and sin offering You did not require.
Then I said, "Behold, I come;
In the scroll of the book it is written of me.
I delight to do Your will, O my God,
And Your law is within my heart."

I have proclaimed the good news of righteousness
In the great assembly;
Indeed, I do not restrain my lips,
O LORD, You Yourself know.
I have not hidden Your righteousness within my heart;
I have declared Your faithfulness and Your salvation;
I have not concealed Your lovingkindness and Your truth
From the great assembly.

Do not withhold Your tender mercies from me, O LORD;
Let Your lovingkindness and Your truth continually preserve me.
For innumerable evils have surrounded me;
My iniquities have overtaken me, so that I am not able to look up;
They are more than the hairs of my head;
Therefore my heart fails me.

Be pleased, O LORD, to deliver me;
O LORD, make haste to help me!
Let them be ashamed and brought to mutual confusion
Who seek to destroy my life;

Let them be driven backward and brought to dishonor
Who wish me evil.
Let them be confounded because of their shame,
Who say to me, "Aha, aha!"

Let all those who seek You rejoice and be glad in You;
Let such as love Your salvation say continually,
"The LORD be magnified!"
But I am poor and needy;

Yet the LORD thinks upon me.
You are my help and my deliverer;
Do not delay, O my God.